Finding Shapes

Squares

Diyan Leake

Heinemann Library
Chicago, Illinois

© 2006 Heinemann Library
a division of Reed Elsevier, Inc.
Chicago, Illinois

Customer Service 888-454-2279
Visit our website at www.heinemannlibrary.com

Editorial: Diyan Leake
Design: Joanna Hinton-Malivoire
Photo research: Maria Joannou
Production: Chloe Bloom

Library of Congress Cataloging-in-Publication Data

Leake, Diyan.
  Squares / Diyan Leake.
       p. cm. -- (Finding shapes)
  Includes index.
  ISBN 1-4034-7476-1 (lib. bdg.) -- ISBN 1-4034-7481-8 (pbk.)
  1. Square--Juvenile literature. 2. Shapes--Juvenile literature. I. Title. II. Series: Leake, Diyan. Finding shapes.
QA482.L436 2006
516'.154--dc22

                                                    2005013859

Printed and bound in China by South China Printing Co. Ltd

10 09 08 07 06
10 9 8 7 6 5 4 3 2 1

Acknowledgments
The author and publishers are grateful to the following for permission to reproduce copyright material: Corbis p. 12 (Craig Lovell); Getty Images pp. **5** (Imagebank/Kaz Mori), **13** (Imagebank/Cyril Isy-Schwart), **21** (Photodisc), **23** (straight, Imagebank/Kaz Mori); Harcourt Education Ltd pp. **6** (Malcolm Harris), **7** (Tudor Photography), **8** (Tudor Photography), **9** (Malcolm Harris), **10** (Malcolm Harris), **11** (Malcolm Harris), **15** (Malcolm Harris), **16** (Tudor Photography), **17** (Malcolm Harris), **18** (Malcolm Harris), **19** (Malcolm Harris), **22** (Malcolm Harris), **23** (cube, Malcolm Harris; edges, Malcolm Harris; faces, Tudor Photography), back cover (cube, Malcolm Harris); Rex Features p. **14** (Dave Penman)

Cover photograph reproduced with the permission of Corbis

Every effort has been made to contact copyright holders of any material reproduced in this book. Any omissions will be rectified in subsequent printings if notice is given to the publishers.

The author and publisher would like to thank Patti Barber, specialist in Early Childhood Education, for her advice and assistance in the preparation of this book.

The paper used to print this book comes from sustainable resources.

Contents

Some words are shown in bold, **like this**. They are explained in the glossary on page 23.

What Is a Square?

A square is a **flat** shape.

It is a special kind of **rectangle**.

4

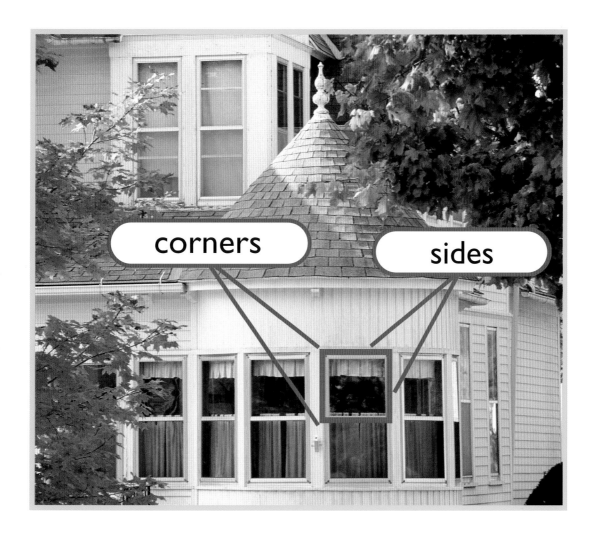

corners

sides

Squares have four corners and four **straight** sides.

All the sides are the same length.

Can I See Squares at Home?

There are lots of squares at home.

Some of them are in the living room.

Some birthday cards are square.

What other squares can you see at home?

There are squares in the kitchen.

Some squares are big and some are small.

There are squares in the bathroom.

The square white tiles are smooth and shiny.

Can I See Squares at School?

There are lots of squares at school.

You can climb the bars in the gym.

These boards have squares on them.

The squares are red, yellow, blue, and green.

Are There Squares in the Park?

This playground is in a park.

There are squares on the climber.

Some of the plants in this park are planted in squares.

Different plants are different shades of green.

What Do Patterns with Squares Look Like?

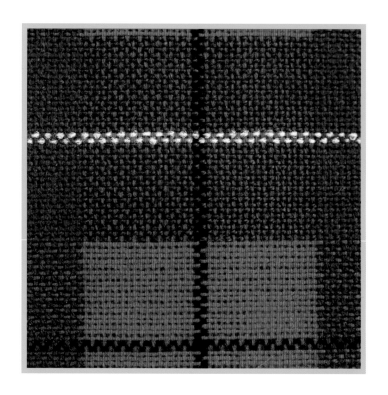

This cloth has a pattern of squares on it.

Cloth like this is used for blankets and rugs.

This board is for playing games.

It has a pattern of blue squares and yellow squares on it.

Can I See Squares on Other Shapes?

faces

You can see squares on a **cube**.

A cube is a **solid** shape with square **faces**.

edges

Cubes have six square faces.

They have **straight edges**.

Are There Cubes at School?

These blocks are **cubes**.

You can make a tall tower with them.

Dice are cubes.

They have spots on each **face**.

Can I Play Games with Squares?

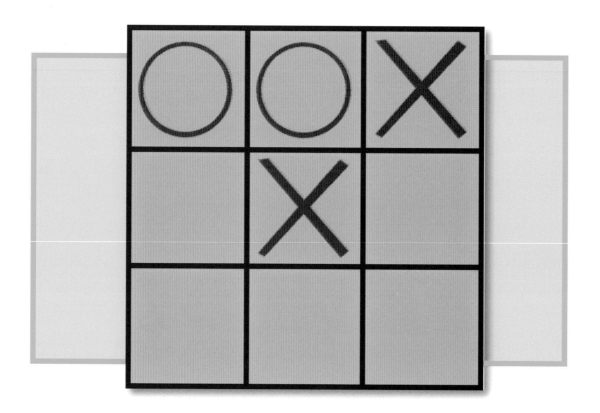

You can play tic-tac-toe with a friend.

You try to get three in a row.

Each domino has two squares with dots on them.

You can set them up and knock them down.

Can I Make Squares out of Other Shapes?

See how many ways you can make squares!

Picture Glossary

 **cube**
shape with six faces that are all the same size

 **edges**
lines where two faces of a shape come together

 **faces**
flat outside parts of a solid shape

 **flat**
having no thickness

 **rectangle**
flat shape with four straight sides and four square corners

 **solid**
having thickness; not flat

 **straight**
not bent or curved

Index

Note to Parents and Teachers

Reading nonfiction texts for information is an important part of a child's literacy development. Readers can be encouraged to ask simple questions and then use the text to find the answers. Each chapter in this book begins with a question. Read the questions together. Look at the pictures. Talk about what the answer might be. Then read the text to find out if your predictions were correct. To develop readers' inquiry skills, encourage them to think of other questions they might ask about the topic. Discuss where you could find the answers. Assist children in using the contents page, picture glossary, and index to practice research skills and new vocabulary.